Original title:
Willow's Wisdom

Copyright © 2025 Creative Arts Management OÜ
All rights reserved.

Author: Alec Davenport
ISBN HARDBACK: 978-1-80566-671-4
ISBN PAPERBACK: 978-1-80566-956-2

Threads of Life in a Whispering Grove

In a grove where secrets thrive,
A tree with tales starts to jive,
Swaying branches, bent with glee,
Whispers like a gossiping bee.

Its leaves hold laughter, bright and light,
Throwing shade, what a funny sight!
With every breeze, it cracks a joke,
Telling stories of silly folk.

Beneath its boughs, the creatures play,
A raccoon steals snacks, what can I say?
Squirrels dance, a nutty ballet,
In this grove, joy keeps gloom at bay.

So come and sit, let laughter bloom,
In this quirky, leafy room,
With every whisper, a chuckle grows,
In nature's heart, humor flows.

Nature's Ancient Counsel

A squirrel once told me to chill,
Don't rush, take your time, just sit still.
Trees have seen all, they know the score,
In silence, they teach us much more.

The breeze giggled, a playful tease,
While dancing leaves whispering with ease.
Nature's charm has a funny way,
Of brightening up a dreary day.

Whispers of the Swaying Grasses

Grasses sway as if to say,
Laugh a little, join the play!
When clouds get heavy, and skies seem gray,
Remember, sunshine always finds a way.

"Why fret?" chuckled the old oak tree,
"Life's a joke, so let it be!"
With roots underground, they all conspire,
To make us giggle, lift us higher.

The Resilience of Twisting Roots

Twisting roots don't take offense,
They wiggle and laugh, it's all just pretense.
When the ground shakes and seasons shift,
They smile and sway, it's their nifty gift.

A wise old rock sat nearby,
Said, "Wobbly? Nah, just reaching for the sky!"
Dance with the wind, let worries go,
Even roots possess a funny flow.

Advice from the Ages in Nature

The mountains chuckled, their peak so tall,
"Don't sweat the small stuff, it's nothing at all!"
Rivers just giggle as they twist and turn,
"Life's too short; just laugh and learn!"

Nature speaks softly, with humor divine,
Baboons and badgers share tales over wine.
So take a lesson from branches and bees,
Laughter is everywhere, carried by the breeze.

In the Arms of Seasons

Springtime giggles, blooms so bright,
Winter's chill, oh what a fright!
Summer's sun, a golden cheat,
Autumn leaves dance, oh what a feat!

Cup of cider, toast the frost,
Trousers wet, oh what a cost!
Nature chuckles, nature pranks,
In her arms, just laugh and thanks!

Veils of Green Serenity

Lush green curtains sway and swing,
In the breeze, the birds do sing.
Frogs in chorus, croak a tune,
Nature's humor, bright as noon.

Squirrel with acorns, hoarding tight,
Hiding snacks, oh what a sight!
Mossy carpets soft and deep,
Tread with care, or take a leap!

Threads of Time in Nature's Loom

Spider spins a wobbly web,
Knitting dreams with every ebb.
Grasshoppers leap, a joyful jest,
Time unfurls, but never rests.

Rabbits bounce, and hedgehogs roll,
Nature stitches, heart and soul.
Each moment woven, laugh and play,
In her fabric, we'll drift away!

The Heart of the Forest Beats

Deep in woods, where echoes swell,
Trees whisper secrets, tales to tell.
Barking dogs and laughing breeze,
Nature grins, puts mind at ease.

Fungi dance and critters prance,
Underneath the mushroom's stance.
With every rustle, giggles tease,
In the heart, there's joy to seize!

The Calm in Chaos

In a storm of socks and shoes,
A calm resides, it gently snooze.
Dancing ducks in puddles splash,
While tea gets spilled, oh what a crash!

Giggles rise amidst the mess,
A blender spins, oh what a guess!
Laughter echoes through the din,
A bright grin wins, let fun begin!

Finding the Path of Peace

In a world of rush and hurry,
Take your time; there's no need to worry.
A snail's pace is just a treat,
With silly dance moves, oh so sweet!

Hopping over, puddles gleam,
On this path, we laugh and dream.
Every twist tells a joke or two,
Join the fun, it welcomes you!

Nature's Gentle Repartee

The trees whisper secrets, oh so sly,
As clouds giggle, floating by.
A squirrel jokes, with acorn snack,
Nature's jesters, no need to lack!

The breeze tickles, makes leaves shake,
Every rustle, a playful wake.
Sunbeams wink, a bright little tease,
In this realm, all hearts find ease!

The Shade of Sturdy Hope

Beneath tall branches, shadows play,
In this refuge, troubles sway.
A chipmunk's laugh spills seeds around,
In cozy shade, joy can be found!

All worries fizzle, pop like gum,
In a world where giggles come.
Grab a friend, come sit right here,
Let sunshine melt away all fear!

The Language of the Old Root

In the garden, roots do chat,
With the worms, and a nearby cat.
They gossip about the birds and bees,
Life's a puzzle, with roots at ease.

Old trees tell tales of days gone by,
While branches wave to the passing sky.
Their secrets hide in twisted bark,
Like a riddle left in the park.

Leaves laugh as they dance in the breeze,
Tickling the air with such playful ease.
Each rustle a joke, a playful quip,
Nature's humor in each little dip.

So if you find yourself feeling blue,
Just listen close, they'll talk to you.
The roots have wisdom, silly yet profound,
In every whisper, joy can be found.

Harmony in the Fluttering Heart

In the meadow, butterflies dance,
Each twirl a quirky, silly romance.
They tickle the flowers, making them giggle,
Nature's comedy, a light-hearted wiggle.

Bumblebees buzz with a cheeky flair,
As if they know secrets, light as air.
"Buzz of the day!" they happily sing,
Bringing a smile with the joys they bring.

The grasshoppers hop with boisterous glee,
A hopping ballet, wild and free.
Each leap a laugh, a jovial start,
Celebrating life, with every heart.

So listen closely when the wind does play,
You'll hear the laughter of a brand new day.
Nature's concert will lift your mood,
As hearts find rhythm in every brood.

Where the River Meets the Sky

The river giggles as it flows,
Winking at clouds with a silly pose.
"Come take a dip!" it softly calls,
Making ripples, where laughter falls.

The fish join in, with playful splashes,
Chasing bright dreams in joyful dashes.
With every flip, they share a grin,
A watery ballet, let the fun begin!

Above, the birds have a frolicsome squawk,
In their own world, they dance and talk.
A chorus of chuckles under the sun,
A meeting of spirits, all in good fun.

So when you gaze at the vast blue sky,
Remember the laughter of the river nearby.
Together they join in a frolicking spree,
Life is a joke—just float, be free!

The Grace of Swaying Grace

In the breeze, tall grasses sway,
Doing the cha-cha, come what may.
Each blade a dancer, oh so spry,
A shimmering giggle as clouds drift by.

Flowers nod their heads in cheer,
As if they share a joke, so dear.
"What do you call a bee with a bad haircut?"
Buzzing with laughter, they wiggle and strut.

The sun smiles down, its rays a tease,
Casting funny shadows through the trees.
Nature's stage is set, the crowd in stitches,
With each gentle sway, the laughter it ditches.

So remember to dance in the softest breeze,
Join in the fun, feel life's tease.
For even the earth knows how to be light,
In every sway, find your own delight.

Fragrant Memories of the Past

In the garden, scents collide,
A pop of lavender, let's not hide.
Grandma's secret pie, oh what a tease,
A slice of humor with a side of cheese.

Rusty bikes and laughter loud,
Spinning tales that make us proud.
Forgotten dreams in daylight's glow,
They dance around like puppets, though!

Old shoes squeak on wooden floors,
Mismatched socks behind closed doors.
With every chuckle from the past,
We toast to days that fly so fast.

Breezy whispers through the trees,
Playful breezes, if you please.
A jester's heart in nature's arms,
Tickles our minds with timeless charms.

Echoes of Tranquility

The pond reflects a laugh or two,
Echoes bounce like kangaroos.
A frog jumps in with quite the splash,
Creating ripples with each mad dash.

Breezes giggle through the reeds,
Whispers taking playful leads.
The sun tiptoes on a leaf,
Cackling softly, beyond belief.

A snail moves with regal grace,
In this slow-motion, funny race.
Nature's moments, pure and bright,
Sparking laughter, a pure delight.

With every breeze, the flowers sway,
Dancing clues of joy today.
In gentle quips, the world's alright,
With playful echoes, take your flight.

The Lightness of Letting Go

A balloon escapes to the sky,
With each new laugh, it flirts and flies.
Old worries pop like soap bubble's glee,
As we giggle at life's mystery.

The burden shrinks with each light chuckle,
Finding joy in every huddle.
Letting go brings a silly grin,
As we shed the weight under our skin.

Like leaves that dance in autumn's cheer,
We twirl and tumble, full of cheer.
Giggles rise, like wisps of air,
Castles of dreams, built without care.

In moments shared, we find release,
Softening hearts, a gentle peace.
Our laughter echoes, light as a feather,
In letting go, we bond together.

Hidden Strengths in the Stillness

Amid the quiet, the wise ones dwell,
Sharing secrets we can't quite tell.
Roots beneath hold stories bold,
Belly laughs hidden in the cold.

In pauses deep, the heart does bloom,
Finding joy in the empty room.
A whisper of a breeze turns wise,
Turning stillness into surprise.

Sitting sounds with giggles true,
Each heartbeat hums a song anew.
In silence lives the loudest cheer,
Embracing strength, we hold so dear.

So let us stand, with roots so fair,
Seeing strength in whispered air.
With laughter's pulse, we grow and sprout,
In stillness, boldness takes a route.

Echoes in the Rustling Leaves

In a dance, the branches sway,
Squirrels gossip, come what may.
A leaf fell down, it tickled my nose,
Nature giggled, look how it grows!

The acorns drop like little bombs,
While raccoons sing their silly psalms.
"Why don't trees make good musicians?"
"Too many roots in their decisions!"

Solace in the Soft Embrace

In the shade, a napping frog,
Dreaming deep, a honking hog.
Trees may frown, but I see smiles,
They're plotting fun, let's stay awhile!

The birds chirp tunes, a silly beat,
Footloose critters dance on their feet.
"Why don't they care about the rain?"
"Because they have no time for pain!"

The Art of Letting Go

A twig released, like a secret shared,
The grass below is quite unprepared.
"Why do leaves fall?" the children ask,
"To have fun and complete the task!"

The wind can't stop its cheeky play,
Whispering jokes, then it flies away.
"What's the tree's favorite dance?"
"The swing, of course! Let's take a chance!"

Guardians of the Gentle Breeze

Bouncing branches form a choir,
Lifting spirits ever higher.
They hum a tune that sounds quite silly,
Makes me chuckle, oh so frilly!

Bugs in hats join the parade,
Dancing in the sunny glade.
"Why do flowers always bloom?"
"To chase away the dull and gloom!"

Beneath the Veil of Green

Under branches, secrets hide,
Squirrels giggle, they don't abide.
Leaves whisper tales of love and jest,
Nature's humor, oh what a fest!

Beneath the shade, I trip and fall,
Laughter echoes, a jolly call.
The world is silly, can't you see?
Join the dance, come laugh with me!

Glimmers of sunlight peek and play,
Wiggling worms have much to say.
Petals flutter, butterflies tease,
Tickling frogs bring merry ease.

In the green, such joy they weave,
Life's a prank, just take your leave.
Beneath the veil, the fun runs free,
Nature's jest is glee for me.

Reflections in the Still Waters

Mirror mirror in the pond,
Who's the funniest of the bond?
A frog in shades, a snail in shoes,
Splashes giggles, what a muse!

Fishy faces, bubbles rise,
Glistening fins, oh my, surprise!
The water sings a silly tune,
Dance with me 'neath the laughing moon.

Wiggly worms play hide and seek,
While dragonflies play peek-a-boo, so chic.
Ripples tease the surface bright,
Nature's comedy, what a sight!

In the stillness, laughter flows,
Every splash the joy bestows.
Reflections ripple, truth is clear,
In this mirth, I leave my fear.

The Dance of the Fleeting Shadows

Shadows prance on midnight ground,
Dancing creatures, oh so profound!
Echoes giggle through the night,
While moonbeams wink in pure delight.

A cat in boots, a mouse in cap,
Join the fun, let's bridge the gap!
Round and round, they twirl with glee,
In this jest, they all are free.

Fireflies join the merry feast,
Lighting up the night's own beast.
Each flicker sends a chuckle loud,
Nature's jesters, oh so proud!

As daybreak comes, they slip away,
With laughter gone, they'll always stay.
In fleeting shadows, joy resides,
In every step, the fun abides.

Stories Woven in the Bark

Bark tells tales, oh so wise,
Of furry friends and silly cries.
In knots and curls, their stories blend,
Whispers of joy that never end.

Beetles joke of evening feasts,
While the ants discuss the least.
A ladybug thinks she's a star,
Staging plays from near and far.

Each ring a chapter, laughter's ink,
Nature's humor makes us think.
Leaves flip pages in the breeze,
Sharing tales with gentle ease.

So gather 'round, embrace the bark,
Where stories live, oh what a lark!
In nature's book, let's write our part,
With every giggle, we share the heart.

Harmony in the Swaying Breeze

In a dance with the wind, they sway,
As if mocking gravity's strict play.
Leaves giggle and spin, what a sight,
Even squirrels join in the light.

Branches whisper secrets of old,
As the sun shines bright and bold.
Birds chime in with cheeky songs,
Sprinkling joy where laughter belongs.

Nature's band, a comedic feast,
In their rhythm, our worries cease.
Every rustle a joke, every twist a tease,
Making life a bit sweeter with ease.

Every Leaf a Story

Each leaf that falls has a tale,
Of lost acorns and a wandering snail.
They gossip in colors, bright and grand,
Like nature's own humor at hand.

One brags of storms it has survived,
While another just wishes it thrived.
They prank the breeze, tickle the sky,
As if planning a surprise on high.

Nature's jesters, full of grace,
With cheeky smiles on every face.
Telling tales of silly events,
Bringing laughter, no need for pretense.

Cradled in the Embrace of Nature

Nestled under branches, cozy and snug,
Nature wraps you like a warm bug.
With a chuckle, the flowers bloom,
They know how to chase away gloom.

The moss winks as you sit by,
While butterflies aim for a pie in the sky.
Every moment feels like a jest,
Nature's humor at its very best.

Frogs croak jokes from their leafy throne,
As the wind hums a melody, overblown.
Laughter flows, it's the main course,
In the banquet of life, let's endorse.

Tales Written in the Sky

Clouds drift like thoughts in a dream,
Sketching comics in a sunlight beam.
They giggle and shift, forming a grin,
Telling tales of where they've been.

Each sunset spills colors so bright,
Painting the sky with laughter and light.
Stars twinkle back with sly surprise,
As if sharing secrets behind their eyes.

Nature's theater; the sky a screen,
With stories of mischief, funny and keen.
Where the moon winks and the comets dance,
In this grand show, we all take a chance.

A Journey Under the Starlit Boughs

Underneath the leafy shades,
A squirrel wears a tiny hat,
He thinks he's King of Glades,
But trips over his own scat.

The stars above, they wink and cheer,
As bugs do the tango, full of flair,
A raccoon juggles chunks of beer,
While owls hoot and toss their hair.

A fox pulls pranks with wicked glee,
Dressing up in socks and shoes,
The turtle's dance is quite the spree,
The rabbit just can't hide his blues.

So here we laugh under the sky,
Where critters scheme and plot with flair,
Each whisper tells a riddle sly,
In nature's jest, we find our share.

The Nurturer's Embrace

In the garden, bugs hold court,
With daisies serving tea,
A dandelion's quite the sport,
Waiting for a bee.

The ants parade in silly hats,
All marching to and fro,
While worms giggle, 'What of that?'
As seedlings put on shows.

A lazy cat observes the scene,
Winks at every little flop,
While birds bust moves, you know what I mean,
To keep the laughter up on top.

In nature's arms, all's a tease,
Where joy and blooms unite,
With every buzz and swaying breeze,
Who cares if plants are upright?

Echoes Among the Dappled Sunlight

Among the trees, a frog croaks loud,
   He thinks he's quite the star,
While crickets make a merry crowd,
   They sing of dreams bizarre.

A badger dressed in polka dots,
   Twirls 'round, proud as can be,
He sweeps away all mundane thoughts,
   And spills his herb-spiced tea.

The chattering birds do join the fun,
With antics that might raise a brow,
They leap and hop until they run,
Chasing shadows, don't know how.

In this sunlight's merry chatter,
Where laughter echoes sweet and light,
Each moment swells, with joyful matter,
   As nature basks in pure delight.

Nature's Timeless Symphony

The tree frogs play a cheeky tune,
With flutes made from old twigs,
The smiling sun hums with a croon,
While ants do their dance on digs.

Butterflies spin like seasoned pros,
In pirouettes, they flit and flair,
The bees compose their buzzing prose,
With rhythms dancing in the air.

A cheeky parrot cracks a joke,
As crickets snap their fingers loud,
While mushrooms poke their heads and poke,
Joining in, they're quite the crowd.

So nature plays, an endless show,
In laughter and in jest we sway,
With every note, our hearts will grow,
As smiles bloom in bright array.

A Tree's Gentle Lament

In the breeze, I sway and bend,
Fighting squirrels that won't befriend.
They laugh up high, I grumble low,
'Get off my leaves, you're stealing the show!'

Roots deep in soil, I'm firmly stuck,
Yet here comes a storm, oh what bad luck!
With branches flailing, I take my chance,
'Is it too late for a tree dance?'

Embracing the Elements of Life

I've seen the sun, I've felt the rain,
Wishing sometimes to join a train.
Chopping wood would make me mad,
But I'll stick around, so don't be sad!

The wind whispers jokes, oh what a tease,
I giggle softly with swaying leaves.
Who said trees can't have some fun?
A little bark always weighs a ton!

Whispers of the Winding Branch

Branching out with puns quite witty,
Be careful, I might get too gritty!
Lichen laughs as it grows so bold,
'Why don't you leaf? You're starting to mold!'

Glimmering dew, the morning's cheer,
I grin and stretch, feeling no fear.
A dance with shadows in full delight,
I'm a tree that's dreaming all through the night!

Secrets Beneath the Bark

What lies beneath? Oh, take a peek,
A ticklish beetle, oh so chic!
In my crevices, laughter reigns,
Who knew that wood could hold such gains?

I hear the giggles of critters near,
Whispers of secrets that I love to hear.
Nature's jokes, my daily bread,
Shouting from branches, 'I'm not dead yet!'

Knowledge Carried by the Wind

A leaf took flight, oh what a sight,
It whispered truths, with all its might.
The squirrels laughed, they rolled on ground,
As wisdom swirled, all around found.

A gust appeared, like a jolly friend,
Tickling the branches, with a playful blend.
The acorns danced, in silly spree,
While knowledge giggled, wild and free.

Breezes brought tales of pies and cheer,
The branches creaked, 'Oh lend an ear!'
With every flap, a chuckle sent,
In nature's joke, all time was spent.

So heed the wind, with its playful glee,
For lessons learned can tickle thee.
With joy it sails, so lift your chin,
And let the laughter drift within.

The Quiet Strength of Resilience

A tree stood tall, proud and spry,
With roots so firm, it reached the sky.
The storms would come, and rain would pour,
Yet still it grinned, wanting more.

The branches swayed, in a funny dance,
Creating shadows, giving chance.
A bird perched high, with jokes to tell,
Of conquering storms, and all was well.

While some trees cracked, and fell apart,
This one just chuckled, with a stout heart.
'Tis all a part of nature's game,
To bend and bow, but not feel shame.

So if you stumble, and laugh you must,
Remember the tree, in the wind you trust.
With each toppled leaf, there's wisdom wide,
Find strength in giggles; it's a funny ride!

Beneath the Canopy of Dreams

Under the leaves, where shadows play,
Silly dreams come out to sway.
A raccoon's mask, a magic hat,
Whispers of joy, where laughter's at.

Beneath the stars, in the midnight hue,
Silly wishes danced and flew.
A dandelion fluffed, in full delight,
Made wishes sprout, taking flight.

In this garden, the moonlight beams,
Everyone shares their funniest dreams.
A frog in pants, a cat in shoes,
Will spin a tale, you cannot lose.

Let's gather 'round, in this leafy dome,
Where giggles echo and jokes feel at home.
For under dreams, joy calls your name,
In this silly world, we all feel the same.

The Nurturer of Lost Souls

In a cozy nook, where shadows creep,
A friendly tree hears secrets keep.
With open arms, it hugs the lost,
And shares a joke, no matter the cost.

"Hey there, friend! Why the long face?"
The tree would ask, with leafy grace.
"Life's a mishap, a tumble and fall,
But I've got laughter—come one, come all!"

With every root, a story spun,
Of mishaps great and jokes begun.
Squirrels shared giggles, while birds would sing,
In this haven, joy is the thing.

So seek this tree, when lost or low,
For it knows well how laughter can grow.
A hug from the bark, a nutty jest,
In the heart of this tree, you shall find rest.

Between the Tides of Time

The clock ticks loud, no time to waste,
My sock's a thief, it's made a haste.
With every wave, the ocean grins,
It knows the tricks where time begins.

Lemons fall from trees, so absurd,
They roll away, thinking they're birds.
I chase them down, it's quite a sight,
Yet they escape before the night.

A seagull swoops with a cheeky peep,
It steals my snack, it takes a leap!
But I forgive, with a hearty laugh,
Nature's comedy, a well-scripted craft.

So here I stand, with sodas spilled,
Between the tides, my spirit thrilled.
The silliest days turn wisdom bright,
We giggle through the soft moonlight.

Lessons in the Flowing Stream

A frog that thinks it's quite the king,
Jumps on a rock, gives a mighty fling.
It slips and splashes, oh what a show,
The lessons here, they just might grow.

The fish complain of their boring fate,
But dance with bubbles, oh isn't that great?
They swirl and twirl beneath the sun,
In water's waltz, they have such fun!

The turtles take their time, it's true,
While diving ducks all speed on through.
Yet wisdom's found in slow, not fast,
We laugh and learn, enjoying the cast.

As laughter echoes off the shore,
Each ripple whispers, "Come explore!"
In every splash, a funny scheme,
Life teaches best in the flowing stream.

Serenity in the Shaded Glade

In a shaded glade, squirrels abound,
Each with a secret, not to be found.
They gather nuts, a furry parade,
Their antics leave us joyously swayed.

A bunny hops, with a wink so sly,
It mocks a bird, attempts to fly!
With floppy ears, it leaps so high,
A fuzzy jester beneath the sky.

The leaves might whisper, "Take a seat,"
While ants in a line march down the street.
The wise old oak gives a hearty cheer,
As laughter in nature's soothing here.

So shade yourself 'neath branches wide,
In funny moments, take great pride.
For every giggle that we parade,
Is wisdom found in the shaded glade.

The Poetry of Endurance

From mountain tops to valleys deep,
A snail crawls forth, no need to sweep.
With laughter loud, it takes its time,
In this odd journey, all's a rhyme.

The ants decide to tackle a crumb,
They hoist it high, making a hum.
With teamwork strong, they make it grand,
In nature's world, they take a stand.

A bear tries yoga, strikes a pose,
While bees buzz by with tiny prose.
In every clumsy twist and turn,
A funny lesson, we all must learn.

Through ups and downs, we'll dance along,
In every blunder, there's a song.
So let's embrace the comical chance,
For life's a wild and funny dance.

Coursing Through Life's Currents

I once met a tree with a quirky grin,
Its branches were dancing, where shall I begin?
It whispered of streams that ran wild and free,
Said, 'Flow like the water, don't forget to be me.'

With roots deep in laughter, it taught me to sway,
'Life's just a party, come join the parade!'
The leaves rolled their eyes, like they knew all the fun,
While squirrels took bets on who'd next win a run.

I laughed at the branches that tickled the sky,
Said, 'Join the wild current, don't just stand by!'
For every deep current has bubbles of cheer,
And paddling hard can still lead to a beer.

So dance like the river, let laughter prevail,
In currents of chaos, you'll always set sail.
With lessons from trees and a mind that's set free,
Just look to the branches, they'll guide you like me.

A Canopy of Silent Stories

Beneath the tall arch of tangled green hair,
Lies a whispering world of much laughter to share.
The branches hold secrets, more silly than sage,
Each rustle and giggle can brighten your page.

A squirrel scampered in with a hat made of leaves,
Proclaiming, 'I've come for the tales some trees weave!'
With twigs as my pen, I scribble my lore,
Of acorn-sized dreams and a roaming uproar.

Their laughter is hidden in sunlight's warm hues,
A canopy swirling in colorful views.
The beetles march forth in a kooky parade,
While ants form alliances, their troops are displayed.

So listen, dear friend, for each breeze has a song,
In stories retold, you'll find where you belong.
Join in with the leaves for a marvelous jest,
In a forest of laughter, you'll surely be blessed.

The Art of Letting Go

In life's great big garden, where hiccups are found,
We learn there's a beauty in falling down bound.
A leaf drifted lightly, it fluttered and spun,
Said, 'Letting go isn't sad, it's just fun!'

I plucked at my worries, like fluff on a chair,
Released them like whispers that danced on the air.
A critter nearby laughed and joined in the show,
Said, 'Isn't it silly how fast we can grow?'

With laughter like bubbles, we twirled all around,
Finding joy in the chaos that life's brought us down.
So hold on to giggles and toss fear aside,
For in letting go, we find life's grand ride.

And when you're all tangled in stress or distress,
Just think of my tale and wear joy like a dress.
For every grand flourish can start with a cheer,
And letting go, darling, is simply more clear.

Sunlight Through the Leaves

Sunlight beams filtered, all sparkly and gold,
Dancing through leaves, like a story retold.
A beam whispered, 'Hey, let's play a good game!'
While bees buzzed along, calling out all our names.

The branches waved joyfully, beckoning near,
'Come join in the fun, shed that worry, my dear!'
In this leafy theater, where nature's so bright,
Even shadows are starlight, making day feel like night.

A chipmunk bolted past, donning shades like a pro,
Said, 'Life's a grand stage where the laughter just flows!'
With sunbeams like spotlights, each moment a thrill,
You'll find joy in the whispers and learn how to chill.

So let's raise a glass, to nature's sweet play,
With sunshine our sponsor, let's frolic all day.
For life, just like laughter, is meant to be shared,
With sunlight through leaves, our burdens are bared.

Stories Told in the Rustling Breeze

In the park where squirrels dress,
They gossip with the leaves, no less.
A nut here, a dance there, all in a tease,
Tales of acorns carried on the breeze.

Birds in the branches plan their chirps,
Practicing lines like tiny little jerks.
With each flutter, a punchline flies,
Who knew that nature was so sly?

Breezes tickle the grass below,
As ants march on their tiny show.
With every snap of twigs, a laugh,
Nature's circus, a funny half!

So if you wander through this space,
Listen closely, find the grace.
For every whisper from a tree,
Holds secrets of absurdity!

A Refuge Among Ancient Trees

Beneath the shade of branches wide,
A raccoon plots with his furry bride.
In their secret lair, laughter and glee,
They throw a comedy jam, just you wait and see!

Mice play charades in the roots so deep,
Hiding from owls who'd rather sleep.
The fox cracks jokes about junkyard cars,
While batty bats strum on imaginary guitars.

Each rustle and cackle, quite a delight,
As shadows flicker; oh, what a sight!
The trees hum along with their leafy breath,
In this refuge where nature laughs with zest.

So come and sit, share a grin,
Find joy that bubbles up from within.
Amidst the whispers and the leaves' gentle tease,
Funny tales thrive, as soft as a breeze!

Wisdom Carved by the Seasons

As autumn leaves tumble, they dance and play,
Old owls chuckle, saying, "What a display!"
Pinecones drop like secrets untold,
Squirrels hoarding treasures worth more than gold.

Winter's chill brings snowballs, quite the fight,
Snowmen grinning 'til they melt out of sight.
Frosty air sparkles with laughter, oh dear!
Snowflakes swirl, whispering winter cheer.

Springtime giggles bloom in bright hues,
Flowers spill secrets as sunlight renews.
Bumblebees buzzing, in search of a tease,
While rain showers sprinkle laughter with ease.

Then summer arrives with its heat and its rays,
Crickets concert beneath the sun's gaze.
Branches sway with the tunes of delight,
Nature's wisdom wraps you tight!

Shadows Dancing in the Moonlight

Moonbeams giggle on the dance floor ground,
While crickets chirp in rhythms profound.
Owls hoot in sync with their feathered friends,
Under the stars, where laughter never ends.

A firefly flickers, plays peek-a-boo,
Chasing shadows, as stars too pursue.
The night whispers secrets, a funny twist,
As sleepytime stories in darkness persist.

Bats swoop low with their acrobat flair,
Creating chaos in the cool night air.
Every rustling leaf joins in for the fun,
While shadows dance under a cheeky moon, on the run!

So if you're out when the day must flee,
Join the dance, oh wild and free.
For in the night, beneath the large sky,
You'll find laughter and joy, oh my, oh my!

The Quiet Grove Speaks

In the grove where squirrels play,
Trees gossip in a leafy way.
A rabbit winks, its ears on high,
While a turtle takes its time to sigh.

Fern and bark exchange sly jokes,
About the acorns and their pokes.
The breeze can't help but join in fun,
Blowing hats from everyone.

Moss chuckles, 'Time to be a rug!'
While frogs leap in a cozy snug.
Underneath a canopy bright,
Nature's laughter feels just right.

So come and sit and tune your ear,
To the dialogue that's all but clear.
In this space where nature thrives,
Even the quiet seems to jive!

A Tapestry of Green Dreams

In a patch of grass, so lush and wide,
Dancing leaves find a place to hide.
A snail slides past with cheesy grace,
While daisies giggle at his pace.

Butterflies flaunt their colorful flair,
Making the bees stop and stare.
'Why fly in chaos?' the flowers tease,
'When you can dazzle with such ease?'

The sun beams down with a cheeky grin,
As hedgehogs roll, socializing in.
A picnic unfolds, crumbs scatter around,
Even ants think this place is sound.

With each blade of grass, a wink, a cheer,
In this tapestry, joy's ever near.
So gather your laughter, come and play,
In dreams of green where we all sway!

Murmurs of the Meadow

In the meadow where daisies thrive,
Grasshoppers play, and bees arrive.
A wind chime laughs, it's quite a sight,
While the sun prepares to bid goodnight.

The dandelions whisper, 'Blow us away!'
While butterflies dance a bright ballet.
Crickets chirp their twilight song,
Singing praises to where they belong.

A cow munches grass, wise and slow,
Thinking deeply of where to go.
'Life's a journey,' says the breeze,
'Take it easy, just like these!'

As shadows stretch, the stars come out,
The meadow chuckles; there's no doubt.
Every creature knows their role,
In this laughter-filled, gentle stroll.

Reflections on a Gentle Stream

By the stream where the ducks do quack,
The water dances, no sign of slack.
Pebbles giggle as ripples play,
Telling tales of the sun-kissed day.

A fish slips by, with a cheeky flick,
Splashing water like a party trick.
Frogs jump in with a belly flop,
Creating waves that just won't stop.

Mossy banks whisper secrets low,
As dragonflies put on a show.
'Transform, dive, and do a twirl!'
They challenge the bugs, who start to whirl.

As starlight sparkles on the stream,
Reflections ripple the night's dream.
The laughter echoes in the night,
In nature's joy, all feels right!

The Comfort of Canopies

Under the leafed embrace, quite grand,
I lost my sandwich, slipped from my hand.
Squirrels chattered with delight and glee,
They laughed as they feasted at my expense, you see!

Branches sway in a whimsical dance,
Not just for shade, but a nature romance.
My worries drift like blossoms in spring,
As I watch the chaos the critters bring!

Tickling the sky, the limbs play peek-a-boo,
They whisper secrets that only trees knew.
A comfy nook, a resting place,
Where life unfurls at an easy pace.

Laughter echoes in the rustling leaves,
Even the bumblebees giggle with ease.
So take a break, find a cozy front,
Under the canopy, life's a silly hunt!

Beneath Stormy Skies

When clouds gather, and raindrops get strong,
I dance like a fool, feeling right, not wrong.
The thunder claps like a raucous crowd,
Mother Nature's humor, fast and loud!

I duck and I weave, splashes all around,
Every puddle's a treasure, that I have found.
The wind, a playful twirl, I must embrace,
While laughing at raindrops that splatter my face!

Lightning flickers, a dazzling show,
The trees soak it in, like a water flow.
Each drop's a tickle, each storm's a jest,
Living life fully, in nature's wild fest!

Giggles erupt in the stormy strife,
Under gray skies, I find my true life.
With joy like a breeze, let worries just fly,
As I dance in the rain, oh me, oh my!

Secrets of the Verdant World

Amidst the greens, mysteries flutter and flit,
The bugs hold council, each one a wit.
'Why did the chicken bring its own chair?'
'To sit on the grass, and avoid all the scare!'

Leaves whisper tales of grand escapades,
Of rabbits with hats and their fruit parades.
A fungi's got gossip, all juicy and ripe,
Sharing the news of their latest type!

The flowers brag, of their colors so bold,
Competing for laughs, as their stories unfold.
Once, a mushroom claimed it could fly at dawn,
But fell on its cap and then sighed, "I'm gone!"

In laughter and mirth, where green things abide,
Each secret shared with a twinkle of pride.
So join in the fun with the critters and buds,
Unravel the jokes of the verdant thuds!

Trials of a Sturdy Sapling

A tiny sapling, standing so tall,
Wobbles and giggles with each little fall.
'Grow up!' shouts the oak, quite wise and stout,
But our little friend grins, 'I'm figuring it out!'

Facing the wind, the sapling sways,
Trying to compose its own silly plays.
The squirrels roll by, with acorns in tow,
"Oh dear, my branches just need more glow!"

Sometimes it shivers when the storm clouds loom,
But it dreams of the day, when it'll burst into bloom.
Yet giggling companions lighten its load,
As laughter rings true in the verdant abode!

So here's to the trials of growth on this earth,
With wiggles and chuckles, oh, what a mirth!
A sturdy sapling, testing its song,
Believing that laughter is where they belong!

Elegance of the Resilient Tree

In a dance of leaves so bright,
The tree sways with delight.
Its branches twist and twirl,
Nature's own graceful whirl.

With roots that ground it well,
It laughs at the winds that swell.
A trunk so strong and round,
It holds its ground, so proud.

In storms, it won't knock down,
Just flicks away its frown.
"Bring it on," it seems to say,
"Tomorrow is another day!"

Even squirrels come to see,
What tricks the tree will decree.
With each twist and every freeze,
The tree just giggles with ease!

Embracing the Wind's Caress

Here comes the breeze, oh what a tease,
It makes the branches sway with ease.
The tree starts to shimmy, shake, and cheer,
"Catch me if you can!" it calls out, dear.

Dancing leaves, in a joyful flight,
Twist and turn, what a silly sight!
The wind chuckles, blows a loud kiss,
While the tree giggles, basking in bliss.

"Hold tight!" cries the tree as it bends,
But with every gust, the fun never ends.
The squirrels hang on, what a wild ride!
Each swirl, each twirl, something new to confide.

"Next time, let's spin faster!" the tree shouts,
Reveling in the laughter that flouts.
With every gust, it sings, it beams,
Together they'll dance, in whimsical dreams!

Budding Hopes and Broken Dreams

Little buds peek from the bark,
Dreams of sunshine, oh how they spark!
Yet a jaybird with a wicked grin,
Swoops for lunch with a flapping spin.

"We'll grow again!" the buds softly chime,
"Just give us a moment, it's all in time."
Yet a gust comes by with a loud "whoosh!"
And off they flutter, like a wild luge!

"Who needs petals?" they giggle and jest,
"Floating downwards, we'll still look our best!"
The earth catches them with an open hand,
"Your dance is beautiful, just as you planned."

In a tangle of dreams, hopes take flight,
Even when lost, they shine so bright.
Each turn of fate, a silly old scheme,
And what's life, if not one big dream?

Starlit Conversations with the Earth

Under a moon that winks and blinks,
The tree talks to the soil, or so one thinks.
"Tell me, dear Earth, why do you sigh?"
"Ah, just thinking of clouds that drift by."

"It's such a circus, this life of ours,"
The tree whispers, reaching for stars.
"Each twig's a decision, and each leaf a cheer,
What emerges from laughter, oh dear, oh dear!"

The ground giggles back, with a shake and a roll,
"Every storm passes, just follow your soul!"
They chuckle and chatter, a silly old pair,
In a dance of deep roots and a moonlit prayer.

As fireflies wink in their gentle gleam,
The tree and the earth conspire a dream.
With laughter and tales that never do cease,
Together they find a moment of peace!

Nature's Portrait of Patience

In the garden, time stands still,
A snail races, what a thrill!
Bees are buzzing all around,
Their dance a sight, a comic sound.

Trees wear crowns of leafy green,
A squirrel's quest, a nutty scene!
Rabbits hopping, tails held high,
While butterflies flirt, oh my, oh my!

Rivers giggle on their way,
Sharing secrets of the day.
Clouds doing flips, a skyward show,
Nature's jesters, stealing the show!

Each moment blooms with laughter's grace,
In this funny, wondrous place.

Branches Stretching Towards Tomorrow

Branches stretch with eager glee,
Trying hard to touch the sea.
A parrot squawks, "I need a drink!"
While turtles pause, they smile and wink.

Leaves gossip in the gentle breeze,
Tickling each other with mischievous tease.
In the sunlight, shadows play,
Pretending they're on holiday!

Ducks are waddling, wearing shades,
As frogs croak jokes in leafy glades.
Squirrels launch aerials for nuts,
In this circus, only fun struts!

Every branch knows just how to grin,
In this symphony of nature's din.

Grounded by the Earth's Love

Roots dig deep in playful soil,
Earthworms chuckle with great toil.
Mice throw parties down below,
While daisies dance and put on a show.

Caterpillars munch with delight,
Dreaming of wings, oh what a sight!
Ants parade, they're quite the team,
All to make the garden gleam!

A rock grumbles, "I'm strong and stout,"
As ladybugs laugh, darting about.
Under the sun, they play charades,
Nature's laughter never fades.

Here the humor of life's embrace,
Brings a smile to every face.

The Promise of Renewal

Springtime giggles at winter's end,
As flowers bloom, they twist and bend.
The sun wears shades, it's looking cool,
While snowmen melt, a wondrous fool!

Frogs in ponds start to croak,
Making puns, it's quite the joke.
New shoots sprout with giddy flair,
As nature sings without a care.

A breeze whirls in, with secrets to share,
Tickling trees with loving flair.
With every bud, a chuckle's grown,
This cycle of life is humor's throne!

In this dance of start and cease,
Nature smiles, and finds her peace.

Beneath the Dappled Shade

In the shade where squirrels play,
I heard leaves gossip all day.
They chuckled softly, flicked their twigs,
And shared their secrets, bold as digs.

A chipmunk danced, a nut in paw,
While trees leaned close, a wise old flaw.
"Life's a game of tag, you see,
But sometimes, hide behind a tree!"

Beneath the branches, laughter soared,
As bullfrogs croaked, and crickets roared.
With every joke, the sunlight played,
In the leafy world, we laughed and swayed.

In dappled light, all worries fade,
With every rustle, a fun charade.
So join the trees in playful glee,
They're wise enough to just be free!

The Whispering Boughs

The boughs above began to chat,
About a frog that wore a hat.
"Have you seen him leap," one said,
"With style too strong, he's seen and fed!"

A breeze swooned low, it heard the joke,
And teased the twigs till branches broke.
"Dear friends, it's hard to beetle on,
When laughter's here and shadows dawn!"

Then came a bird, with feathers bright,
"What's so funny? Oh, what a sight!"
The whispers grew, a merry band,
With every rustle, they took a stand.

Embrace the breeze, ignore the gloom,
For all who gather here can bloom.
There's wisdom found in every chuckle,
Under boughs where joy won't buckle!

Secrets of the Swaying Tree

A tree swayed gently, laughed with joy,
Telling tales of a dancing boy.
"He spins around, his arms are wide,
Oh, to be free like him!" It sighed.

With every creak, the branches sighed,
"Don't take life too serious, just glide!"
A squirrel piped up, so bold and spry,
"I prefer to scamper, oh my, oh my!"

Secrets whispered in rustling beats,
Of mismatched socks and silly feats.
"Why be serious? Come, let's twirl!"
Sway the tree and give joy a whirl!

So join the dance, don't hesitate,
For giggles can make hearts ornate.
In every sway, a smile will be,
Within the secrets of the tree!

Lessons from the Weeping Branches

The branches wept, but not with sorrow,
Instead, they laughed at a duck's tomorrow.
"Quacking on, he thinks he's grand,
But who knew ducks could dance on sand?"

The tears would fall, but not in gloom,
They sparkled bright, like flowers in bloom.
"Wipe your eyes, take life in stride,
There's so much fun on joy's wild ride!"

Puddles glimmered, reflections made,
With every laugh, the worries frayed.
"Dance in the rain, let laughter rain,
Life's a splash; don't fear the stain!"

Lessons flowed from those branches wise,
Revealing joy with each surprise.
In laughter's wake, we all would find,
The beauty of a playful mind!

The Dance of Time and Leaves

Time waltzes beneath the trees,
Leaves tickle the ground with ease.
They swirl and spin in a merry show,
While squirrels stand guard, ready to throw.

The sun joins in with a cheeky grin,
Playing peek-a-boo, letting fun begin.
Each rustle and giggle brings laughter near,
As branches sway, shedding not a tear.

Nature's mirror reflects our own,
As we dance on paths seldom known.
Together we flit, laugh, and twine,
In this garden of chuckles, all is divine.

With whispers of breeze and a soft, sweet nudge,
Even the shyest leaves begin to judge.
"Why not join in?" they bubble with glee,
"Come, let us twirl, wild and free!"

Rooted in Resilience

Deep in the earth, where the snacks are found,
Roots giggle softly, all snug and bound.
"Oh look at us, we are quite the charade,
Holding together this grand leafy parade!"

With each storm that brews, they chuckle aloud,
"Bring it on thunders, we'll make you proud!
We've seen a few winters, a drought or two,
We dance in the soil—oh, what can't we do?"

A tiny seed joins, unsure at first,
"Will I be strong or will I burst?"
"Fear not, dear sprout, we're all in this game,
We're strong, we're silly, we'll never be tame!"

So with strength underground, they tell tales of fun,
Of digging and stretching, and racing the sun.
For life is a dance, with roots as our shoes,
Waltzing through troubles, with laughter we choose.

Silhouettes of Strength

In the twilight glow, shadows leap and bound,
Far from the struggles, they frolic around.
"Oh look, I'm a giant!" one shadow boasts,
While another descends, playing host to the ghosts.

With flickers of light, they perform on the wall,
A circus of shapes, can you hear the call?
"Join in the fun, let's twist and turn,
With every odd angle, there's magic to learn!"

The trees watch in awe, as the silhouettes play,
"In our stillness, there's laughter that sways.
So let's sway and dart, keeping spirits high,
Strength isn't just holding, it's letting hearts fly!"

So under the starlight, they birth giggles anew,
Forms of the brave, and colors askew.
In dance and in light, they embrace the night's song,
Silhouettes of strength, where none can be wrong.

Soft Shadows of the Soul

The soft shadows flutter, all cuddly and sweet,
With secrets and giggles as they frolic and meet.
"Let's play hide and seek in the light of the moon,
I'll cover my eyes, and you hum us a tune!"

They tiptoe through memories, both gentle and bold,
Weaving together the warmth of the old.
"Oh, remember the time we danced on the breeze?
With whispers of laughter that rattled the trees!"

In this whimsically whispered embrace of the night,
The shadows conspire in playful delight.
"Let's glide through the dreams, oh, what can we find?
A canvas of chuckles where hearts are entwined!"

And so they frolic, the shadows of cheer,
Lifting our spirits, banishing fear.
In the soft, gentle quiet, they sing their old song,
For shadows are laughter—this is where we belong!

The Gnarled Guardian's Tale

In a grove where branches sway,
A tree spills secrets every day.
Squirrels gossip, birds all chime,
It's a circus of nature, oh so sublime.

A wise old trunk with knots so neat,
Claims it knows the dance of feet.
"Just wiggle, jiggle, do the jig,"
And watch the critters leap and dig.

Laughter lingers in the breeze,
As rabbits twirl among the leaves.
Frogs croak in rhythm, what a sight,
Underneath the moon's soft light.

So next time you find a shady nook,
Listen close, and you'll find the hook.
Nature's humor, wild and free,
The best punchlines hide in trees!

Beneath the Shade of Solace

Underneath the leafy dome,
Where creatures gather, far from home.
A turtle snored, a spider spun,
While ants organized their next fun run.

A picnic of giggles, crumbs, and snacks,
The raccoons plotted mischievous acts.
"Let's steal the bread and blame the cat!"
Oh, the joy in their playful chat!

A beetle raced with panache and pride,
Challenging birds to join the ride.
While a wise old owl stirred in his sleep,
Dreaming of jokes that made him leap.

In the refuge of green, laughter flies,
Under shady canopies, joy multiplies.
So heed the whispers of trees above,
For life is richer when shared with love.

Echoes of Nature's Embrace

In a forest where whispers play,
Echoes of laughter dance and sway.
A pesky fox with a cheeky grin,
Claims he can outsmart the whole din.

"Tell me a riddle, I dare you to!"
Challenged a crow in feathers of blue.
The trees laughed softly, their leaves confide,
As secrets turned into giggles that glide.

A chipmunk chimed in with a twirl,
"Who can out cheese me? I'm quite the girl!"
And while the animals clapped and cheered,
Even the shyest critters appeared.

So let the echoes ring through the air,
Of delighted hearts, a joyous affair.
In the arms of nature, sorrow erases,
Smiles and giggles fill all the spaces.

Lessons from the Weeping Bough

There's a bough that droops with grace,
Hiding tales of an old tree's face.
"Don't take life so seriously," it cried,
As the breeze tickled and teased, it sighed.

"Oh, join me, friend, don't be a bore,
Bounce like a branch, let your spirit soar!
Every drip and drop holds a jest,
So share your giggles, it's for the best!"

The leaves rustled, giggles abound,
As squirrels leaped, chasing sounds.
"Life's too short to frown and mope,
Just twist and shout — that's the best hope!"

So next time you feel down and gray,
Find a bough where laughter stays.
The world is comedy, if you see,
Dance with the branches, and set your heart free.